DRA

SPAC

Robin Hawkins

Battle-Cries

Songs & Humour
Poems and Prayers
with the Occasional Monologue
for the Disciple who wants to do
Battle!

Many of these songs may be
listened to at
www.robinandjulie.co.uk.

Robin Hawkins can be contacted at robinvmh@outlook.es

europe books

© 2023 **Europe Books**| London
www.europebooks.co.uk | info@europebooks.co.uk

ISBN 9791220145978
First edition: December 2023

Battle-Cries

To Julie, my partner in life, ministry and song; my warmest encourager; my most helpful critic; and my best friend; without whose support, so many of these "verses" would never have seen the light of day.

Many Thanks to Marialaura, Elisa, Rachele, and all the staff at Europe Books, for all their support and ready help in bringing "Battle-Cries" to print.

*"You rule my life,
Its daily chores,
My job by You is run.
So why should I join the union,
When I'm the Chairman's son!"*

"The Chairman's Song"

Index & Themes

Preface 13
BATTLE-CRIES 15
Don't You Know That There's A War On? 15
Occupy The Land 17
We're God's Band of Men 19
The Enemy Within 20
We're All Where It's At! 22
The Minister's Lament 24
It's Our Church 26
Where You Are 30
I Need You 32
Jeremiah's Song 33
Worship – A Way Of Living 35
Come To The Meeting 36
Denial 38
Religion Individuate! 39
The Camel Song 41
My Song 43
Complete In You 44
Sparrow 45
PRAYERS 47
Please Change Me 47
Touch My Heart 49
Within It All 51
You Bless Me! 53
You're A Friend 55
Benediction 56

CONVERSATIONS WITH FATHER GOD	57
I Love You Anyway	57
BATTLE-CRIES	59
A Problem More Deadly Than Aids!	59
FOLLOWING JESUS	61
Could You Look?	61
I Wouldn't Mind Him – But…	63
LOVE	65
Henry's Bride	65
PRAYERS	66
Adore You	66
Give A Man A Vision	68
Through The Eyes Of Jesus	70
Speak The Word	71
In His Name	72
The Parable of the Hosepipe	73
The Song of the Hosepipe	74
Too Small	76
Lord, When You Are Near	77
PRAYERS	79
Helpless	79
PRAYERS	81
More Of You	81
In His Eyes I'm Beautiful	83
A Plea For Christ-mas	85
Stranger Than	87
The Wonder Of Christmas	88
The Parable of The Peanut Nibblers	91
The Joy Of My Salvation	92

Wandsworth Prison Non-Blues...93
CONVERSATIONS WITH FATHER GOD.................95
Introspection...95
He Sent His Son To This...97
If I Believed 99
LOVE 100
Julie's Song 100
We've Forgotten How To Die 101
Keep The Peace...102
LOVE 103
By Your Love...103
Nicknames..104
Living Word 106
Mr. Average 107
Go Free...109
The Chairman's Song..111
Will You Be My Child?...112
Getting Younger..113
His Name Is I Am 115
Martha, Mary 117
Talking Evolution Blues 119
The Prickly Hedge 122
Walk On The Water 124
Things Start Happening 126
Still The Hungry Die 128
Talking Hey Bert's Got Religion Blues.................................130
Gentle Waters..132
The Barrel Song 133
It's So Good 135

So much to sing 136
You Were Made For Me 138
A Gentle Plea For Tolerance 139
The Bride 140

Preface

By

J. David Pawson

"Singers and Seers. The church today has many singers but few seers. Even fewer combine both gifts. Those that do, echo the prophetic musicians in the Bible. Men like Samuel and Elisha. Women like Miriam and Deborah. Above all King David and his choirs.

They saw things as God saw them. They felt his feelings. They used poetry and song to get past heads and into hearts. The lyrics were short, sharp and even shocking. Through them, living truths confronted dead traditions. The God of yesterday became the God of today, getting his people ready for tomorrow.

Robin and Julie have received a burden from the Lord. They are using their particular gifts to communicate it to his people. With devastating honesty, they expose our weaknesses – what an inspiration to call our denominational labels "NICK" names! They are not afraid of humour, or even satire. Yet there is no malice. Behind the public chuckles are private tears. They stab us from the inside!

Nor is there despair. The mourning turns into dancing. The God of today is doing a new thing. These songs are not calling us to look back in anger, but to look forward in anticipation. If you read and listen carefully, you will hear a fresh call to become part of a united people ready to reoccupy the land in the name of the Lord.
I think you will enjoy this book of poems and songs. Even if you don't, it's likely to do you just as much good!"

BATTLE-CRIES
Don't You Know That There's A War On?

Don't you know that there's a war on?
Can't you see we're in a fight?
Look around the battle's raging -
With the darkness and the light!
It's a battle of two kingdoms -
It's a struggle to the end.
Both are locked in mortal combat,
Neither one will freely bend.

Don't you know that there's a war on?
It's a battle in the air.
It's invisible to human eye-
Yet raging everywhere!
You can see the devastation-
The invader leaves behind.
The broken lives, the sorrow,
Sickness, sin of every kind.

But we've got the means of winning,
We could put the foe to flight.
Yet our army's in confusion-
And it's lost the will to fight!
The soldiers just want comfort -
And a quiet civilian life.
They like to wear the uniform,
But back off from the strife.

It's because the outcome's certain,
And the victory is ours.
That we're tempted to complacency-
Against these evil powers.
For although their back is broken -
There's a sting still in their tail.
And if we don't keep our guard up,
They can wound us where we fail.

We may not have understood it,
When we first were born again.
For there's more than we had bargained for -
In learning how to reign.
It's where forceful men will take it -
That the Kingdom will be found.
And it's only as we make him,
That our enemy gives ground.

So we can't escape the conflict,
Unpleasant it may sound.
For it's only overcomers -
In the Kingdom will be crowned.
We must put aside distractions-
All our lethargy and fears;
And join the ranks of battle;
As the final victory nears.

Copyright ©1984 Words & Music By Robin Hawkins

You can listen to "Don't You Know That There's A war On?" at www.robinandjulie.co.uk

Occupy The Land

There's a castle on a hill-top -
Ruling over everyone.
You can hear the soldiers singing-
Of the battle that's been won.
The enemy's defeated -
From the country he'll be banned.
Tomorrow we'll be moving out-
To occupy the land.

There are still a few small pockets -
Of resistance here and there.
But they will soon be mopped up-
Come the morning - never fear!
Tonight we'll talk of victory -
And how we'll make a stand.
Tomorrow we'll be moving out -
To occupy the land.

Yet it's sheltered in the castle -
We feel safe behind its walls.
Let's stay awhile, the foe will-
Still be there when duty calls.
There's nothing much that he can do -
To thwart the things we've planned.
Tomorrow, we'll be moving out-
To occupy the land.

And so the victors rested,
While they pondered dreams of heaven.
The enemy could scarce believe -
The chance that he'd been given.

Marshalling his forces,
For the final coup he planned.
Tomorrow – let them come -
Today we'll occupy the land.

Eventually the soldiers looked out -
From the castle walls.
The enemy was everywhere -
He looked so strong and tall.
Retreating back instinctively,
They dropped the campaign planned.
The enemy would never let them -
Occupy the land.

The evil grew on every side-
It spread on every hand.
The soldiers were surrounded-
They gave in to its demands.
And now they're pleading for their lives,
Because they'd failed to stand.
They'd failed to take their victory -
And occupy the land.

We're so often like that castle -
In our churches all so fine.
Yet the enemy's advancing-
Let's move out while there's still time.

Remember he's defeated,
He must yield at our command!
Today we must move out as one -
And occupy the land.

© Copyright 1982 Words & Music by Robin Hawkins

You can listen to "Occupy The Land" at
www.robinandjulie.co.uk

We're God's Band of Men[1]

We're God's band of men!
Each one born again,
Each one committed to the battle for our land.
It won't be an easy job,
Going after Satan's mob-
He's had it all his own way now for far too long!

So we're marching in to occupy the country,
Satan's defeated, he surrenders on demand!
Mighty strongholds, broken of their long holds,
Fall before us at the Lord's command.

It isn't even proper war,
Jesus Christ has done it all.
Defeating Satan's armies at Golgotha long ago.
It should be merely mopping up,
Wherever he keeps cropping up.
But no-one's tried to stop him, he's had time to grow.

So we're marching in to occupy the country...

© Copyright 1982 Words by Robin Hawkins

---

[1] This song was inspired by David Pawson (who else?!) He was describing a group of bovver-boys who had come to Christ and were all ready to take the battle straight to the enemy!
I always imagined singing it to an old marching tune from the Baptist Hymnbook!

The Enemy Within

It is not the other army -
Who can be the greatest foe;
It may not be the guns of battle
That destroy our ranks below.
Nor yet the charge of cavalry,
The fearful noise of steel;
The pounding of the horses hooves-
Their one desire – to kill!

No, there is one more dangerous-
Than the enemies outside;
You expect to have to fight them
For they're on the other side.
No, the one that's far more lethal,
Who will never let you win;
Is the one that's not so obvious-
It's the enemy within!

There are those who are among us -
Who appear to be so right;
With a charm that is deceptive
But who live by human sight.
They think the way that men think,
Moved by fear in all they do;
Who haven't learnt to see life yet -
From Father's point of view.

We've often blamed the Sadducees -
For watering down the Word;
But all around are those who act

As if they've never heard.
Who've been taught until they're bloated,
Know the Word from A to Z;
Yet it's never touched their heart-
It's all stayed in their head.

We live in such a mixed up world-
Where truth no more shines through;
And things that may be true for me
Are not thought true for you.
Where men dilute the Word of God,
'Til it's just mere advice;
Who dwell upon the "comfy" parts -
Avoiding those not nice.

When Ezekiel looked for someone -
Who would stand inside the gap;
He never thought the day would come
He'd have to guard his back!
But now the Lord looks for the ones,
Who hate this devious sin;
Who'll stand up straight, be counted -
'Gainst the enemy within!

©Copyright Robin Hawkins 1982

We're All Where It's At!

We're using all the latest lingo,
Really up to date – by jingo!
Though we haven't seen much sin go -
We're all where it's at!

Oh yes, we're really getting with it,
Someone's got a word – they give it.
Never mind the way to live it -
We're all where it's at.

For us renewal's quite the thing!
As long as change – it doesn't bring.
We're happy just to talk and sing -
About it all the time.

We know that each one must be filled,
And as disciples really drilled!
As long as we keep getting thrilled -
We'll stay where it's at!

We're growing very charismatic,
Not to mention theocratic!
Hope we don't all get fanatic -
We're all where it's at!

For us renewal's quite the thing!
As long as change – it doesn't bring.
We're happy just to talk and sing -
About it all the time.

Instead of hymns that often bore us,
Now we sometimes have a chorus!
Someone's even strumming for us-
We're all where it's at!

In this church we're really free,
Rejoicing in our liberty!
Someone's raised a hand I see-
Revival's where we're at!

For us renewal's…

©Copyright 1982 Words & Music by Robin Hawkins

You can listen to "We're All Where It's At" at www.robinandjulie.co.uk

The Minister's Lament

I went to Bible School a brand new creature,
I said to them I want to be a preacher.
I can share that Living Word -
In a way that's understood,
And I feel the call of God to be a teacher.

But I was wet behind the ears and all unwary,
When first I set my foot in seminary.
But what happened to my zeal-
That excitement fresh appeal,
It was quickly buried in that cemeta…seminary!

But yet without a lot more complication,
I soon acquired the needed qualification.
Then I found that people rate us,
The respect due to our status,
But I'm not convinced for such there's justification.

But it was useful when I found my first appointment,
Though quickly I was in for disappointment.
When I told them "I'm a teacher", -
They said, "Great! – Just let it feature,
In the midst of all the rest of your appointments."

For firstly there is all the visitation-
To do before you write each dissertation.
Then there's all the other work-
That you really mustn't shirk.
If you're going to build your reputation.

So now I do the pastoring and business,
The youth work and repair work are my witness.
While the members fill the pews -
I have to keep them all amused,
But for teaching now, I've very little fitness!

So very soon, I'm going to have a break-down -
My name outside's the first thing that they'll take down.
It's a break for which I've yearned!!
I have longed for, and I've earned!
And without me this place will be closing straight-down!

© Copyright 1983 Words & Music by Robin Hawkins

You can listen to "The Minister's Lament" at www.robinandjulie.co.uk.

It's Our Church

"It's my church," said the minister,
Looking out across the pews;
"I feel that I'm only one round
Here who *should* be used.
I'd like to see – in time
– some others play a part -
After three years Bible School,
then maybe they could start
By handing out the hymnbooks
On the door as folk come in,
Then later they could graduate
To take the offering.
We really must be careful though,
Things don't get out of hand
I don't want anyone to think
That I'm not in command."

"It's our church," cried the Deacons,
As they held their monthly court-
Pontificating lengthily in turn,
But saying nought.
"It's such a shame the business-
Always takes so long to say,
That at the end we're left
With very little time to pray!
The radicals among us
Really have to be restrained!
Conservative traditions-
Must be faithfully maintained!
Don't rock the boat, or do a thing,
To cause the slightest stir;
And always to majority decisions
We'll defer."

"It's our church," claimed the people,
As they sat in long debate
"A show of hands says everything –
Our will, they indicate –
On matters of importance such as
where the children sit,
On cups of tea, and flowers,
And whether candles should be lit;
On who will run the garden fete,
And how we put the pews;
On outings in the summer,
And which resort we'll choose.
We're really such an active church,
So busy and alive –
It seems to us there's little here
We really need revive!"

"It's ours," complained the lady
As she shook hands at the door.
With all these new folk joining,
It's not like it was before!
I wouldn't mind them if they'd only leave things as they are,
Instead of trying to lead new-fangled singing with guitar.
Such things are of the devil - only organs play what's sound!
In any case, it's all we've ever used since I've been round.
Occasionally, a piano adds a more informal touch
As long as we keep singing those old hymns we like so much!

"It's our church," cried the Youth Group,
As they brandished their guitars,
"If things are gonna move round here,
They'll need a group like *ours!*
The focus is on youth today,
Young people with a will.
The rest are unimportant -
They're all way beyond the hill.
They never understand us
When we say we want things *real*.

They never seem to worry much
About the way we feel.
They dig their heels in firm
When talk of change is in the air;
If they'll not give us what we want
We'll just stop coming here."

"It's ours!" The charismatics prayed,
In various different tongues!
"It's clear to see throughout the church
That we're the spiritual ones!
The minister's a write-off -
– always sitting on the fence!
The deacons dare not make a move
lest they should give offence.
Praise God, we've got the answers.
Hallelu' we've got it right!
But why do people always seem
To shy away in fright?
It can't be that they're second-class,
Or anything like that.
It's just that they've not made it
To the stage that we are at!"

"It should be My church," mourned the Saviour,
On the steps – outside!
"If I could just get near enough,
I'd woo them as a bride.
I had such plans for how …
… We'd spend our life, year after year;
But plans turn into dreams
That finally fade and disappear.
It hurts to go on loving seeing so little in return.
It's pitiful to see them all-
So filled with self-concern –
Falling so far short of all
- I wanted them to be:
One in love, forbearance,
Peace, and sweet humility."

© Copyright 1980 Robin Hawkins

You can listen to "It's Our Church" at www.robinandjulie.co.uk.

Where You Are

Where is it I'll find your people?
Where is it I'll find your church?
Is it there where I see that steeple?
Where is it that I have to search?

Look past stony walls to open hearts.
Look for those you'll see of kindred mind.
It's a living thing of which you're part,
Each life and mine entwined.

Chorus:
For where you are is where I am,
Where I am, there you are.
Together we will grow up shining -
As the Morning Star;
Together we'll shine as the Morning Star.

You don't need to be large in number.
You don't need preacherman or priest.
Nor even buildings that encumber,
Nor traditions long deceased.

For you are not an institution
Well-entrenched and hard to move
You're a living constitution
Built and ordered by my love.

Where two or three of you are dwelling,
Sharing life around my Son.
There, my Spirit will be welling-
Up in the midst of everyone.

Give to me an open heart;
That wants to listen to my Word.
And I will show each one his part
In how we're going to win my world.

Though you now seem so imperfect,
There's no-one lovelier to me.
I see you as you will be one day – perfect
No spot or wrinkle will there be.

© Copyright 1981 Words & Music Robin Hawkins

You can listen to "Where You Are" at www.robinandjulie.co.uk.

I Need You

As the day needs the dawn – so I need you.
As a picture must be drawn, I need you.
As the river to be free -
Needs to flow down to the sea -
To be all that I should be – I need you.

As a piano needs a player – so I need you.
As my spirit needs prayer, I need you
And if people are to see -
The Lord Jesus, then we -
Must agree that it won't be without each other.

Bridge:
Together, we are Jesus where we're living
We're all that folk will see of Jesus there
Resting in the love that frees us
Living out the life of Jesus
Doing all that He'd have done had He been here.

As a finger needs a hand – so I need you
As I need two legs to stand, I need you
In His Body by His grace
We've our own appointed place
And for all to see His face
I need you
I need you
I need you.

© Copyright 1981 Words & Music by Robin Hawkins

You can listen to "I Need You" at
www.robinandjulie.co.uk.

Jeremiah's Song

You might think I'm knocking -
At the church like all the rest.
For few folk see us now -
As little more than but a jest.
And so our family's pilloried,
And mocked on every hand.
For people see no meaning -
In the things for which we stand.

It wouldn't be so bad -
If they'd rejected godly truth.
But they've not had a chance to see -
That vital living truth.
For we've buried our eternal life -
Beneath our dead tradition.
The hard dry outer crust…
… Now puts it past all recognition.

The structures we've invented -
Are so much our own design.
And why should God revive those things-
So clearly not divine!
For if His Spirit were to leave,
The church should fall apart;
Yet as things are, we might not know -
If He were to depart!

So you can say I'm knocking -
But it's not the sheep I blame.
For we're the folk through whom -
God wants to set the world aflame!
I'd knock the things that hold us back,
From all that we could be;
Rigid structures that prevent -
His Spirit being free.

I'd knock the lack of vision-
I'd knock our temporal goals.
Faithless teaching, leaving us -
Still paddling in the shoals.
The stranglehold on ministry,
Caused by a one-man band;
Unwillingness to change -
That we might reach out to our land.

The love of God's a burning -
Passion, jealous for His sons.
Wanting nothing but the best -
For us His chosen ones.
He grieves to see us hindered,
By the things that hold us bound;
So yes, I'll go on knocking -
'Til they crumble to the ground.

© Copyright 1981 Words & Music by Robin Hawkins

You can listen to "Jeremiah's Song" at
www.robinandjulie.co.uk.

Worship – A Way Of Living

Sometimes when I gather with Your people,
And join with them in songs of sweetest praise;
I have to ask if all the words I sing so easily,
Reflect the way I live on other days.

I've told more lies in church-
Than I dare think of,
Words of hymns roll glibly off my tongue;
Prayers so vague -
– forgotten just as soon as they are said,
Empty words to empty lives belong!

Worship has to be a way of living.
It's more than words we merely say or sing.
It's hour by hour obeying, serving, giving;
It's putting Jesus first in everything.

But in a life of walking with my Jesus,
It's good to meet with those -
Who love Him too;
To give Him thanks with hearts so full -
Of gratitude and praise,
Encouraging each other as we do.

He begs us lay our lives upon the altar,
A living sacrifice is but His due;
Daily dying to our own ambitions and desires,
Is worship that's acceptable and true.
Worship has to be a way of living...

© Copyright 1981 Words & Music by Robin Hawkins

You can listen to this song at www.robinandjulie.co.uk.

Come To The Meeting[2]

On Monday there's Men's Fellowship,
On Tuesday, Women's Own.
On Wednesday, our young marrieds meet,
On Thursday, Groups at home.
Friday's practice for the choir.
Saturday's the Gospel hour -
Hallelujah Sunday's blessed!
It's busier than all the rest!

Come, come, come to the meeting,
Give everyone a greeting,
I'm sorry it's so fleeting,
But I've got another meeting -
And I'm late already now!

We like to open with a hymn,
Followed by a prayer.
The reading next, another hymn,
There's decent order here!
We're not bound by the Prayer Book –
Non-Conformist to the core.
We're free to hold each meeting -
as we've always done before!

---

[2] (*I used to attend a church in Scotland, and one Sunday attended seven different meetings!*)
Whatever happened to the Day of Rest?

Meetings? – we come really-
For the blessing we can get;
We'd never think of giving one,
And so we've never yet.
Our minister's so good,
we leave the work all up to him.
Our only contribution -
will be singing with the hymns.

Meetings – all the best -
Revolve around the notices,
We've such a busy programme -
That we need to know what's next
Each time we come, we take our place –
Just where we always sit!
Any who dares to take it -
Gets left boot of fellowship!

He came that we might have meetings –
Have them more abundantly.
It might not quite be what He said,
But it's how it seems to be.
Yet the strangest thing in meetings -
Is not meeting anyone.
All we see from where we're seated -
Are the backs of everyone!

© Copyright 1980 Words by Robin Hawkins

You can listen to "Come To The Meeting" at
www.robinandjulie.co.uk

Denial

Words…
The pretty syllables –
Rushing out into the smiling air,
Full of joys that promise Him the earth -
That promise Him…
That nothing else now matters;
Foe and friend alike
Can go, disappearing like a woken dream,
For nothing else now matters.
And in the centre stands the One,
To whom I've given all;
And fearing no-one,
Stepping out to tell the world
About a love so great
That I will never understand it!
For who is there can stand against me?
I'll stand alone with He –
Who stood alone for me.

That was - until today…
When faced by those -
Who laughed,
And cursed His Name-
In all the muck and filth of man…
And I just stood there -
Speechless!

© Copyright 1971 Robin Hawkins

Religion Individuate!

I often wonder why it is,
That on occasions such as this:
- A Sunday, once a day of rest -
We all appear in Sunday best!
And don a very different air -
To that which normally we bear.
The reason? – after much research -
Is merely that we've "Come to church!"

It seems we like to feel we've been,
So, slipping in the back unseen:
We sit upon our favourite pews -
And carefully mind our P's and Q's.
With no wish to participate -
Alone and incommunicate…
Religion individuate!

With manner dictatorial,
And faces so censorial:
Voices inharmonious -
And stances sanctimonious;
We carry on our little act -
Forgetting just one tiny fact;
That God knows all that's counterfeit.
He's not impressed – one little bit!

It really would be quite unknown,
If we behaved like this at home:
Where family sees us as we are -
And airs don't get us very far;
Nor need we, knowing our Papa -
Accepts us just the way we are.

A family, one must assume -
Should be a place in which there's room…
To be myself amid the clan,
Accepted just for what I am.
In spite of warts and faults - secure,
Because of Father's love – I'm sure.
No longer weakness need conceal,
But need be only what is real!

© Copyright 1980 Robin Hawkins

The Camel Song

(Well it might have been if the camel could sing!)

You may think that I look like a camel.
You may think that I look rather odd.
Though some find it witty-
To blame a committee-
For the way that I look - I blame God!

They call me a ship of the desert.
I suppose that's my funnel behind.
But I like oases -
And other such places -
With Perrier Water to hand!
(Anachronistic reference to an old TV ad!)

I feel like a beast of great burden.
Have you seen what they put on my back?
Such mountains of straw -
If they put just one more -
Well, I think my whole body would crack!

And as for this eye of a needle;
I've never heard nothing so daft!
Not a thing could I do -
That would help me get through -
For I'm carrying far too much draught.
(Well, you called me a ship!)

I suppose if you tried to unload me;
And I got down and bent all my knees.
I might then get by -
I might pass through the eye…
…But it couldn't be done with great ease.

I suppose if the load I was bearing,
Was pride and resentment and sin.
You would have to unload me -
Or you'd never goad me -
Through door of God's Kingdom - and in.

But how would it be when I got there?
When rid of my load I got through?
With that weight off my back
And my nose in a sack -
Of new grain
- Well I know what I'd do.

I would follow the Master who'd fed me.
Who helped me to shed all that weight.
For what seemed impossible
Now seems no great lossatall
Ah! What a most heavenly state!

© Copyright 1982 Robin Hawkins

My Song

It is never those
For whom life smoothly flows.
Who grow to be so strong,
Deep in their Lord belong.
But those who fall – it's true!
So many times – yet who,
When broken, tired, in pain,
Get up, Go on again.

No, it is never he,
Whose life is problem-free.
Who plumbs those depths of grace,
Strong arms of love embrace.
But he who's known despair
The blackest nights of fear…
…Yet held on – come what may
To see the breaking of the day

We'd like life filled with ease
Each day all joy and peace
But all such hopes are vain
There's no growth without pain!

No, it is never those,
For whom life smoothly flows.
Who grow to be so strong,
Deep in their Lord belong.
But those who fall – it's true!
So many times – yet who….
…When broken, tired, in pain,
Get up, Go on again.

© Copyright 1980 Words & Music by Robin Hawkins

You can listen to "My song" at www.robinandjulie.co.uk.

Complete In You

Thank-You that I'm complete in You, Lord,
I need nothing more.
For I've found when I'm fulfilled in You, Lord,
Problems aren't so big anymore.

Thank-You for every situation,
You're in control.
I know it's all for my salvation,
I'm so glad You're making me whole.

Now we're both agreed,
You know what I need,
Before I start to plead,
That I may be freed,
From some little test.
That's for the best.
I know You want me blessed,
So in You I'll rest.

Thank-You for every situation,
You're in control.
I know it's all for my salvation,
I'm so glad You're making me whole.

Thank-You that I'm complete in You, Lord,
I need nothing more.
For I've found when I'm fulfilled in You, Lord,
Problems aren't so big anymore.
Problems aren't so big as before.
You really make them all look so small.
You certainly do!

© Copyright 1979 Words & Music Robin Hawkins

You can Listen to "Complete in You" at
www.robinandjulie.co.uk.

Sparrow

Sparrow, Sparrow, has no-one seen you there?
Shivering in the cold soaked by the rain.
Sparrow, sparrow, does anybody care -
If you should die, or if you should be in pain?
And who could blame you for thinking in that way?
You're so many and you all look just the same!
And who would put a price on you of more than half a penny?
If you should die, there's always many more.

Sparrow, sparrow, has no-one seen you there?
Searching barren ground to find some grain.
Sparrow, sparrow, does anybody hear?
- Your plea for help, or heed your cry of pain
Sparrow, sparrow, ruffled feathers in the wind,
Who'll protect you from the rain and cold?
I feel your brown eyes follow me,
Appealing for some care;
A sea of faces all like you, and crying -
"Don't you know that we are here?"

Sparrow, sparrow sleeping on the streets at night!
The city's millions cannot hide your plight.
Your Heavenly Father hears your cry,
He longs to dry your tears,
But so many look away and pass on by.

Sparrow, sparrow, do you see Him working there?
Comforting and healing those like you.
Sparrow, sparrow, He's proved how much He cares;
He left His home to share your life with you.
And though His folk are few and sometimes hard to see;
We're growing in His love and power each day;
And in that love we'll carry on,
The work that's He's begun;
To show there's none outside His love,
Important in His eyes is everyone.

© Copyright 1978 Words & Music by Robin Hawkins

You can listen to "Sparrow" at www.robinandjulie.co.uk.

PRAYERS
Please Change Me

Please change me!
Please change the way I am and re-arrange me.
Please do what I can't do and please exchange – the
Wilful, stubborn side of me,
For the heart of Him -
who died for me..
Please change me!

Please take me!
Please make me more like Jesus, don't forsake me!
Even if at times you have to shake me…
Don't give up on me please, go on,
I'll not stop trying to follow on,
I'm wholly yours, but you must come -
And take me.

I'd do it if I only could,
I've tried so hard, but it's no good!
My only hope is if you'll come and ...

Mould Me,
Please mould me in the way you've often told me!
Please make of me a vessel that will hold – the-
Crystal water from above,
That moves my heart with Jesus' love.
Please send your Spirit like a dove,
And mould me, And take me,
Please make me more like Jesus,
Re-create me,

Please do what I can't do and oh, please take me! I'd do it if I only could,
I've tried so hard but it's no good
My only hope is if you'll come and...
Change me, And make me, And mould me,

© Copyright Words & Music by Robin Hawkins
Recorded for Battlecries in 2023.

You can listen to "Please Change Me" at www.robinandjulie.co.uk.

Touch My Heart

Touch my heart!
Then you'll get right through to me.
Touch my heart,
Maybe then I'll start to see -
And understand in more than theory -
Truths that often fail to cheer me,
For they're not yet living
Really in my heart.

Touch my heart!
Maybe then I'll start to change.
Touch my heart!
Maybe then you'll fan the flames -
That so often merely smoulder -
Making my heart so much colder -
Than should be.

I can sing with great expression,
Of the wonders that I've learned.
But they'll never change the way I am
'Til in my heart they're burned.

So touch my heart!
There you'll find the real me.
Touch my heart!
Or I'll be left in poverty.
Oh please open up my eyes -
Give me power to realise,
May Your love right from the start -
Move from my head down to my heart,
I don't want to love in part…

So touch my heart,
Touch my heart,
Touch my heart.

© Copyright 1982 Words & Music by Robin Hawkins

You can listen to "Touch My Heart" at www.robinandjulie.co.uk.

Within It All

I want to trust you, Lord,
But sometimes, when the darkness gathers round -
And almost overpowers me;
It's hard to see your hand within it all.

I want to love You, Lord,
To know You as a generous and open-handed Father,
Showering Your love upon me,
In ways that I can see and understand.

But when, it seems, You take from me,
The things I value most;
The warmth within Your family,
My friends, my fond ideals,
It's hard to see Your love within it all.

Father, O my Father, I may not understand You
But I trust You;
And in Your tender arms I'll rise
Above the problems that would try
To overwhelm me.

Father, Oh my Father,
Though I may not feel it -
I just know You love me;
And in the warmth of Your great love -
I'll rest, believing You'll let nothing,
Ever harm me.

But though it hurts when You expose,
The layers that cover up my weakness;
Thank-You that You care enough to do it,
Thank-You that You care enough to do it.

Now with eyes no longer blind,
Within it all at last I see -
And understand Your love;
Not by lavish gifts,
But by the time You spend with me,
Changing me,
Making me,
Into something precious – like You
Like You.

© Copyright 1976 Words & Music Robin Hawkins

You can listen to this song on www.robinandjulie.co.uk.

You Bless Me!

I learned it early on
That in my weakness lies Your strength;
And yet it's taken me 'til now
To find out what that meant.
For when I'm at my weakest
Feeling drained and full of sin –

You bless me – unearned and undeserved
But still You bless in ways-
That know of no reserve
But why You bless me -
- It's so much more then I deserve –
I'll never know!

I'm glad at last I've seen my worth
How little I deserve;
I'm glad, at last, I've seen in truth
How little I can serve.
I'm sure there must be others
Much more usable than me –
-- And yet…
You bless me…

I know I'm nothing special,
And I have to ask, "Why me?"
Yet I get so encouraged
Used in helping others see.

It seems you do Your work
In spite of all that we may be;
All You seek is a willing heart

In which Your Spirit's free
Empty of self-confidence
Relying on You alone,
-- And yet…
You bless me…

© Copyright 1982 Words & Music Robin Hawkins

You can listen to "You Bless Me!" on
www.robinandjulie.co.uk.

You're A Friend

You're a Friend.
Not one who stands aloft,
Exacting hard obedience;
But one, who seeing me struggle,
Is prepared to come and help;
To come and help,
And You don't mind dirty hands!

You're a Friend.
A friend of sinners,
Who longs to meet my need;
Giving strength that fills my weakness,
Making of me all the things;
All the things,
The things I need to be.

How often I've imagined,
You've a big stick in one hand;
The other with a list -
Of all the things that I can't stand.
But You're a Friend!
One who understands me,
More than I myself.
To whom with open honest heart,
I can say just what I feel;
Just what I feel
For You're a Friend.

©Copyright 1979 Words & Music by Robin Hawkins

You can listen to "You're A Friend" on
www.robinandjulie.co.uk.

Benediction

May your life be filled with all the joy -
That comes from knowing Him;
May thanks abound in all that comes your way.
May you know and do our Father's will -
Each moment of the day,
May you know His Spirit's strength -
When you obey.

And may those who look upon you -
See your life's a different style,
May joy and great contentment-
Light your face up when you smile.

May you walk in such a way -
That you'll bring honour to our King;
May it be your aim to please Him,
Bearing fruit in everything.
May His love be poured out through you -
Drawing folk from near and far;
May the beauty of the Lord of Life
Shine out in what you are.

And may those who look upon you -
See your life's a different style,
May joy and great contentment -
Light your face up when you smile.

May His love be poured out through you
Drawing folk from near and far;
May the beauty of the Lord of Life
Shine out in what you are.

© Copyright 1982

Adapted by Robin Hawkins from Col 1:9-11

You can listen to "Benediction" on
www.robinandjulie.co.uk.

CONVERSATIONS WITH FATHER GOD
I Love You Anyway

*Don't you understand -
I love you anyway?
I would your heart could grasp..
Just what that means.
There's nothing new about you,
I don't already know,
I love you, and accept you -
As you are.*

Why cover up those things
You want me not to see?
Why make me think
You're better than you are?
It's not as if I'm blind -
To all those faults that spoil you so;
I see them but it doesn't change a thing.

But the look that's in your eyes -
Is so uncertain.
And doubts obscure -
A longing to be free.
Because I've shown you more-
Of what you're really like inside,
You think I won't accept you anymore.

But still you're hanging back,
And still you keep away;
You say that you're not worthy -
To draw near.
But can't you see it's only pride -
That makes you feel that way?
It's really just yourself you can't forgive.

© Copyright 1978 Words & Music Robin Hawkins

You can listen to "I Love You Anyway" at www.robinandjulie.co.uk.

BATTLE-CRIES
A Problem More Deadly Than Aids!

Imagine a world that was dying of AIDS,
Or other such deadly disease.
And symptoms that gradually kept getting worse,
Were killing us all by degrees!

Like all things, in time, we get used to this plague,
And the worst of its bouts we are braving.
But things that are socially not very nice -
We don't like to own up to having!

So we pretend that it just isn't there,
We choose to believe we're all right.
But still it keeps killing us one at a time -
For nobody puts up a fight!

Imagine if someone came up with a cure,
That would heal us for good of this virus.
You'd think that the thought of being free from the curse-
Of this plague, with thanksgiving would fire us!

Instead we hear protests – "We're perfectly fit,
There's nothing the matter at all.
We're well as the next man, and mustn't complain-
If we need you to help – we'll call!"

The height of frustration this surely would be,
A cure to kill death at one blow.
Yet people kept dying because in their pride -
There was no-one who wanted to know!

But the virus is real, infecting us all,
It's always caused death where it's been!
It's highly contagious and no-one's immune -
It's something the Bible calls 'sin'.

The cure is Christ Jesus, let everyone know;
For where sin is, death quickly pervades.
But can we be cured if we'll first not admit -
We've a problem more deadly than Aids?!

© Copyright 1983 Robin Hawkins

FOLLOWING JESUS
Could You Look?

How often do we hear the call -
To turn away from sin?
Those who've known a deep repentance -
Seem so full of joy within.
But we can't work it up inside us,
Righteous strictures make things worse.
But the Spirit shows our hearts -
How much our sinning Jesus hurts.

Could you look and not be broken -
By the hurt look on His face?
Could you know that He still loves you,
Without weeping at His grace?
Could you know you're still accepted,
Still your Father, still His child?
That He'll take, and of your worst mistakes -
Make something that's worthwhile.

Peter looked, and uttered,
"Leave me, Lord, I'm full of sin!"
The adulteress looked, and heard the words,
"No more I thee condemn!"
No big sticks, harsh words, condemnation,
Could make more sure of their salvation.
T'was only kindness, love, acceptance –
Broke them, brought them deep repentance!

Jesus never told us -
To convict the world of sin;
But sent His Spirit like a sword -
To search the hearts of men.
He said we're to forgive, accept,
Lest we should stumble too,
For in accepting, not rejecting,
we will see His love win through.

Could you look…?

© Copyright 1980 Words & Music by Robin Hawkins

I Wouldn't Mind Him – But…

I don't mind Pete as such,
although he always talks too much!

You'll always see him up there at the front.
I'd like him to be quieter, and a little more politer;
I wish he wasn't always quite so blunt!

But Peter's very loyal, not afraid of work or toil,
He's a leader in the making, given time.
Faith that's in a child, no deceit and unbeguiled;
Open-hearted, generous and kind.

I try avoiding Paul; he's always on about his call,
I'll be glad when next he goes off overseas!
I find him so persistent, not to mention inconsistent;
As though he's trying everyone to please.

But Paul's so full of zeal, stemming from a faith so real,
He's bold with courage never known to fail!
For each church, he's full of care, spending so much time in prayer;
He's had to suffer many an ordeal!

As for Matthew, Well, I mean,
You simply don't know where he's been!
And you can't rely on such a doubtful past.
(Smugly) Perhaps I shouldn't say it,
But I know you'll want to pray it - through..
I wonder sometimes if it's going to last!

Matt's a different man to long ago when we began,
Now he quietly does his work each day.
He's a man who's seldom seen,
But he's faithful and he's keen -
To do the Father's Will, come what may.

When I think of you-know-who,
Well I know it may be true!
But when he's around I never feel at ease.
And you'd think – Heaven's above!
that for all this talk of love -
He'd choose himself some better men than these!

People insecure will often tend to cast a slur…
On others - just to make themselves look good.
If you've never walked in light,
Then it can be a blinding sight -
Seeing someone live -
The way you know you could!

© Copyright 1980 Robin Hawkins

LOVE

HENRY'S BRIDE

She was taken from his heart to be loved by him.
From underneath his arm to be protected by him.
Not from his head to rule him,
Nor from his feet to serve him;
She was taken from his side to walk beside him.

Bone of his bone, she is part of him.
Flesh of his flesh, she is one;
United by the Spirit's love -
That binds their hearts as one;
No longer are they two, but now they're one.

United in direction, they will move as one.
United in their purpose, they will act as one;
Each dependent on the other, each is incomplete alone;
Drawing strength from one another, they return it.

This is just a pale reflection of a wedding that's to come.
Soon we'll see the bride
That's being prepared for God's own Son.
A bride resulting from the blood
That from His side ran free;
A rib was all that Adam paid,
A broken heart paid He.
She was taken from His heart...

© Copyright 1980 Words & Music by Robin Hawkins

(Adapted from Matthew Henry's Commentary on the creation of Eve)

You can listen to "Henry's Bride" at
www.robinandjulie.co.uk.

PRAYERS
Adore You

I love You for the way when I need help, You're always there.
You always listen, always hear my prayer.
No matter how I feel, somehow I sense You understand,
I love knowing I'm accepted as I am.

I love You for the way You always greet me with a smile.
You're interested in all I try to do.
I love You for the joy I find in knowing answered prayer;
I love the joy of resting in Your care.

But Father, it seems to me my love is so self-centred.
It's governed by the things You've done for me.
Yet Lord, I want to rise above myself and think on You,
Love You, and worship You, for everything You are.

But even so…
I love You for the way You write Your law upon my heart.
I love the way Your yoke is light to bear.
I love the way You've set me free to be myself in You
I love the way You draw me ever near.

Yet Father, it still seems to me my love is too self-centred
Still governed by the things You've done for me.
For Lord, I want to rise above myself and think on You,
Love You, and adore You, for everything that's You.

So lift me Father, lift me
'Til I see Your glory shine.
'Til soaring past those peaks of praise
'Til lost in wonder, I just gaze
on You;
Your light, Your goodness,
Your power, Your purity,
For then may everything in me,
Adore You!

© Copyright 1978 Robin Hawkins

Give A Man A Vision

Chorus: If You give a man a vision,
You give a man decision.
He knows with great precision
What he's aiming for!
If you give a man a goal
You'll satisfy his soul,
It's something that he'll know
Will be worth straining for.

1. Those who aim at nothing much -
   Will always score a bull.
   Those who're going nowhere -
   Have already reached their goal.
   Those who lack direction -
   Can take any path they choose,
   Those who're lost already -
   Have got nothing more to lose.

   But… if You give a man a vision…

2. The preacher tells us in the Word -
   That goals are things to cherish.
   That where there is no vision clear -
   That folk will surely perish.
   God's plan for us is written there -
   For those who want to know it;
   Who're not content to hear the Word,
   But really want to do it.

   So…If You give a man a vision…

3. We drift along in confidence -
Assured of our salvation.
But ignorant of our calling -
And the needs that grip our nation.
We know we're building something,
But we're not sure what it is;
Nor how we should be doing it –
It'll be <u>some</u> edifice!

Yet if You give a man a vision…

Words & Music by Robin Hawkins © Copyright 1981

Through The Eyes Of Jesus

Chorus:
Through the eyes of Jesus -
I can see you clearly now.
Through the eyes of Jesus -
There's no need for hiding now.
As Jesus sees you, so would I -
With no rejection in my eyes;
Through the eyes of Jesus,
There is love.

V.1 Sometimes things get distorted,
Using eyes that are my own;
And all I see, relates to me
And the way I feel alone.
For in my brother, all I see -
Are our different points of view;
His faults and hang–ups look so great -
And mine so small and few.
Chorus

V.2 But in Jesus, we're accepted,
To be ourselves we're free;
In each other, now another
Child of God, I see.
We're still the same but something's changed
Now you're a part of me;
For through the eyes of Jesus
There is love and harmony.

© Copyright 1976 Words and Music by Robin Hawkins

You can listen to "Through The Eyes of Jesus" at www.robinandjulie.co.uk.

Speak The Word

Speak the Word!
It comes from the Lord of Heaven.
Make it heard!
It is full of power to work -
Word for Word!
It is power in those forgiven,
It makes livin' really livin',
And it drives off all misgivin'
Speak the Word!

All authority is His,
At creation it was this -
That brought the planets into being -
Brought the world that we are seeing -
To exist.

Speak the Word!
It is Jesus' Word that rules –
Make it heard!
He's given it to us –
Don't be deterred.
We can learn at Jesus' school,
That His Word's a mighty tool.
Those who see it work are those -
Who'll stand and speak it.

Those of this fraternity,
Whose hearts are in eternity;
Will learn such creativity,
They'll see the Word emerge.

© Copyright Robin Hawkins 2022

In His Name

In His Name we can act with great authority.
Over every power we have superiority.
In His Name we rule with no inferiority -
So – why don't we?

In His Name we can tell the seas to hold their peace.
And tell the wind and rain the moment they must cease.
We can tell the bread and fishes that they must increase -
So – Why don't we?

Why don't we use the power that He has given us?
If He'd been right here today,
And we'd seen Him work this way
We'd have done it when he said to have a go!

In His Name the demons flee with great ferocity.
We can drive out every power with great velocity.
We can stand against each evil and atrocity -
So – Why don't we?

Why don't we do the exploits that He said we'd do?
If He'd been right here today, and we'd seen Him work this way
We'd have done it when he said to have a go!

In His Name there is no-one that's incurable.
There is nothing we might need that's unprocurable.
In His Name we can ensure the unensurable -
So – Why *don't* we?
So – Why *won't* we ? ***Do*** as we've been told!

© Copyright 1982 Words & Music Robin Hawkins

The Parable of the Hosepipe

A certain man had a hosepipe with many branches, and he laid this hosepipe in his garden, and used it to water the dry ground in the lawns and flower-beds.

As time went by the different outlets of the hose became clogged with dirt, and the flow of water slowed until it became just a trickle, and from some dried up altogether.

Now the ground became dry and hardened. No plants grew there and it was barren. So the garden cried out for water, and the gardener heard its cry, and turned up the water once more.

But still there was only a trickle and so he increased the pressure. This cleared the blockages from some of the outlets, and they burst forth with streams of water, but bearing more than they were supposed to, for they were also bearing some of that water intended for the other branches.

But they were few in number, and the garden still cried out for water, so the pressure in the hose kept on building up, until at the points where it was weakest, cracks appeared, and the water flowed out in all directions onto the thirsty ground and its thirst was quenched.

When the blocked nozzles saw what was happening they became angry and said to the Gardener: "We are the appointed channels for watering the garden. Stop up these leaks therefore that the water may pass through us only."

But the Gardener said to them:

"I made and fashioned you as water outlets for my garden, and you had every opportunity to quench the ground, but you would not. Now in holding back the flow, you have made the pipes burst and the water has found other outlets. For be sure of this:

MY GARDEN WILL BE WATERED".

© Copyright 1981 Written by Robin Hawkins

The Song of the Hosepipe

God has lent an ear to His children
and their prayer,
As it's risen on every hand,
God has reassured us,
He's completely overawed us
At His readiness to move in our land.
His life-giving waters are so ready to pour,
His wind's going to come with a mighty roar -
Let's be all prepared and waiting
So that we can move at His command.

God has said His people are His church –
It's not the steeple!
We're the channel of His hand,
A pipe for a fountain, that's enough to drown a mountain
That's going to quench the land.
Now although the Lord has turned the pressure up,
And you'd really think
The whole thing would erupt -
Yet all that's coming out
Is just a trickle on the thirsty ground.

Well, it looks as if some mud is in there
Holding back the flood
And it's just blocking up the spout.
For though the pressure's growing
That holy hosepipe isn't flowing
And the Living Water can't get out!
Though to some will be unthinkable, I fear the worst,
That old and brittle hosepipe is a-going to burst!
There'll be Living Water everywhere
Except in that immovable spout.

Well, the moral of my story is so very salutory
Don't you try to stand against the stream
For God will surely do it
And I know that we would rue it
If in doing so we missed His scheme.
Don't be jealous if you see the waters leak elsewhere,
Be grateful that at least the streams are flowing there!
Come on in the water's lovely
Just be certain that your nozzles are clean.
Don't be jealous if you see the waters leak elsewhere
Be grateful that at least the streams are flowing there!
They will flow wherever you are,
Just be certain that your nozzles are clean!

© Copyright 1982 Words & Music by Robin Hawkins

You can listen to "The Song of the Hosepipe" at www.robinandjulie.co.uk.

Too Small

Too small, to be merely my servant,
Too small, to restore Israel.
I'll make – You a light for the nations,
To bring my salvation-
Through all of creation -
To the uttermost ends of the earth.

1. Kings will arise, and will stand in Your presence.
Princes bow down and Your greatness proclaim.
Because of our God, who is loyal and faithful,
You are the One, He has chosen by name.

2. When I show favour, I'll hear you and answer.
When you need saving, I'll give you my aid.
You'll make a new covenant for the people,
Freeing the captives, releasing the slaves.

3. Though just a remnant of little importance,
Now you will be far too small for your land.
The children you bore in the time of your suffering,
Ask for more space as they grow and expand.

© Copyright 1995 Words & Music by Robin Hawkins
Adapted from Isaiah 49:7-20

Lord, When You Are Near

Lord, when You are near,
Faith replaces fear.
Nothing seems so dear,
As knowing You are here.

Chorus
Lord, it's Your presence we desire-
Your glory and Your holy fire,
If only we could lift You higher-
Bring more honour to Your Name.

When we're near to You,
There's nothing we can't do.
With You we will break through,
Your power and glory too.

So come into this place,
In overwhelming grace.
And let us see Your face,
Your awesome love embrace.

© Copyright 2002 Words & Music by Robin & Julie Hawkins
Music by Sue Morrison

PRAYERS
Helpless

Selwyn Hughes used to talk about the Death & Rebirth of a vision. "Helpless" tries to explore this principle.

Helpless!
So long I've known without Your power
I'm helpless.
Without Your Spirit's moving me
I'm fruitless.
But somehow I've kept pressing on regardless;
Hoping that the things I did -
That You'd bless.

Helpless!
It's more than theory now I know
I'm helpless.
Now everything I try to do seems
Pointless.
Without Your Spirit moving me
I'm lifeless;
And all my efforts come to nought -
Are useless!

Somewhere down the line, the vision died;
In hopeless yearning, longed for it to come.
But like a grain of wheat
That fell into the ground and died
It reappeared when every hope was gone.

Waiting;
There's nothing I can do now Lord, I'm waiting.
I'm sitting at Your feet,
Anticipating.
To know Your inspiration,
Meditating,
For the prompting of Your Spirit,
Lord, I'm waiting…

Prayerful
I feel Your Spirit's burden now
I'm tearful
I see Your face more clearly now
I'm cheerful.
To know Your presence near me Lord's so gracious
Your Spirit's moving in my heart's so wondrous
To move out in Your sovereign power miraculous
Walking in Your radiant light all glorious
Knowing I can't help but be victorious.

© Copyright 1980 Robin Hawkins

PRAYERS
More Of You

Once I heard You tell a friend,
To ask for what she would.
I wondered what, if in her place,
I'd ask for if I could.

The sights and sounds around me,
Burst like bubbles in the air.
So much becomes so little
When I try to draw them near.

Chorus:
So I just want more of You, Lord –
More of You in every way.
I just want more of You, Lord,
In my whole life every day.
I want You to increase in me
That all can see You there
And all the things that are of me
To quietly disappear.

For You're the source of life itself,
The rest will come and go.
In You, I've such abundant wealth
More than I'll ever know.

Chorus:
So I just want more of You, Lord –
More of You in every way.
I just want more of You, Lord,
In my whole life every day.
I want You to increase in me
That all can see You there
And all the things that are of me
To quietly disappear.

Postscript
One thing have I desired of the Lord
That will I seek after
That I may dwell in the house of the Lord
All the days of my life
To behold the beauty of the Lord,
To inquire in His temple.
And behold the beauty of the Lord (Ps 27:4)

© Copyright 1981 Robin Hawkins

In His Eyes I'm Beautiful

Looking through the world's eyes
Looking on the outside,
What do you see in me?
Nothing of attraction
But self-dissatisfaction,
That certainly.
But I've met with a Man,
Who has shown me that He can -
Change me where it counts -
From the inside out,
And make me lovely.

In His eyes I'm beautiful!
In His eyes, I'm precious.
To Him, I'm worth dying for,
That's His kind of love.
He's chosen and blessed me!
With His love caressed me,
And now, He is filling me -
With His kind of love.

Looking now through His eyes
Looking to the inside,
He's teaching me to see.
Your beautiful potential
But one thing is essential:
Set His Spirit free.

To heal your self-rejection,
And give you His perfection,
To change you where it counts
From the inside out.
And make you lovely.

*In His eyes you're beautiful
In His eyes, you're precious
To Him, you're worth dying for
That's His kind of love.
He's chosen and blessed you
With His love caressed you,
And now, He is filling you
With His kind of love.*

© Copyright 1982 Words & Music by Juliet Hawkins

We were on our way one day to minister at Pentonville Prison. While Julie was waiting for me to arrive at our meeting point, she asked the Lord, "Robin has written all our songs, Lord, and I've not written any. Could I not write just one song that we could use? Within 10mins, she had this song, "In His Eyes", and she sang it that evening. It had a powerful impact; over a tense crowd of inmates. But she'd asked for only one song – and that's all my talented wife ever got!

A Plea For Christ-mas

Look at all the decorations,
All the endless preparations,
For a day of celebrations,
What's it all about?

Good news for everyone, you say,
For God has shown His love today,
In putting on our mortal clay,
Become like one of us.

To save us from a lonely death,
The pain of Hell's own fiery breath,
The knowledge that no hope is left,
Is the reason that He came.

This must be, for you and me,
The finest news indeed.
That God should care, is really near,
To save us in our need.
It's something great to celebrate -
With joy and reality.
And overawed, we'll bless the Lord,
For His nativity.

Yet almost everywhere I look,
I find that Christ has been forsook,
And Christmas has a bleaker look,
He's nowhere to be found!

Without Him there's no celebration,
Outside Christ no liberation,
We're still lost in condemnation -
Where's the party now?

No point in getting out the streamers,
'Til we know that He's redeemed us,
Up to then we're simply dreamers -
Hiding in the sand!

But there's still time, His love divine,
Still beckons everyone.
If you'll decide this Christmastide,
To kneel before God's Son
We'll have something great to celebrate -
With joy and reality
And overawed, we'll bless the Lord -
For His nativity.

Copyright© 1980 Words & Music Robin Hawkins

Stranger Than

Stranger than the strangest legend folklore handed down;
Deeper than the deepest love that ever gained renown.
Greater than the greatest sacrifice man ever made,
Was my Lord, who, to win Himself a bride, His life He paid.

Nowhere do we find in all the stories ever told;
No romantic minstrel ever dared to be so bold.
Never has a con-man tried a more unlikely yarn,
Than that of the Creator dying for those who meant Him harm!

Easier it would be to think that we're all here by chance;
The belief that God's a spaceman doesn't make such great demands.
Simpler to accept what's right for you is not for me,
But still the truth outshines the fiction – harder though it be.

Had I wanted to invent God, He'd be more acceptable;
Not one who asks obedience, who accepts no less than all.
Who challenges me to die to self that I might truly live,
Yet promises that more than I could ask, He wants to give.

But it's not as if the story ends at
Saving us from sin;
It would have been enough to know
We'd always be with Him.
But who'd conceive the heights -
To which He longs to lift His own,
Not content with us as servants,
He shares with us His throne!
Not content with us as servants,
He shares with us His throne!

© Copyright 1981 Robin Hawkins

The Wonder Of Christmas

What's happened to our sense of **wonder**?
- That ability to be amazed by the unexpected;
Awestruck by the unfamiliar.
"**Wonder**" that is: Surprise mingled with admiration and curiosity –
- We've lost it.
No… **wonder**. No **wonder**!

We're in a world that has turned its back on God.
That chooses to believe in anything but Him.
It's an irony that some are filled with **wonder** at His creation,
Then cover it up with an incredible statement of faith –
"It just happened!"
People no longer fear God;
They're no longer awed by Him,
But rather, try to reduce Him to a figment of our imagination -
that leaves us with nothing at which to **wonder**.

But that won't make Him go away!
He is the God who is there!
The One who called into being –
The **wonders** of this universe;
Who has fixed His love Upon – A speck of cosmic dust called
- Earth.

There's a world in that speck – our world –
Full of even tinier organic cells –
Microcosms of life called humankind.

A **wonder**-full creation!

Amazingly – God knows and loves each such
microcosm of life.
How can He?
Why should He?
We can only **wonder** at it.

Christmas is when God became flesh
Contained Himself in one such microcosm
To reach this fallen world.
STOP!
Let the **wonder** of this fill you!

These microcosms have their own social order
(We might **wonder** why they bother!)
But God sees even that!
He told the lowest and the highest that He'd come, –
shepherds and kings!
No-one was too good for Him;
And no-one was too bad.
Don't you **wonder** why He took the trouble to do so?
The shepherds **wondered** at it;
And everyone they told **wondered**.
Mary **wondered** what it all meant.
Wise men ***worshipped!***

But Christmas is full of such **wonders**:
Angels bringing messages from the Infinite One - Who fills
the Universe;
Angelic Choirs filling the skies,
Stars appearing to order,
and to guide,
A virgin becoming pregnant!
A King born in a stable!
The sign of the manger:
Deliverance from death threats!
Dreams, Visions, Protection!

And yet the **wonder** of it all:
The God-child was born to die (at the God-ordained time) –
And **wonder** of **wonders,**
to rise again from the dead!

That we, mere microcosms of life
Might live forever,
And know the love of the
Infinite One,
Who cannot be contained by His Universe.
Let the **wonder** of all that happened that first
Christmas
Fill you again, and again, and again.

© Copyright 2018 Robin Hawkins

The Parable of The Peanut Nibblers

Once upon a time, a king gave a great banquet to which all were invited - as many as wanted to come. As people congregated in the outer rooms they enjoyed a drink of new wine, and nibbled at peanuts. There were some however who were quite overcome at their own unworthiness to be invited. They looked at their clothes and felt they were much too shabby to be worn to a banquet. But they didn't realise that the king had given each guest a new set of clothes. Others were so impressed by the sumptuous surroundings that they thought that this was the feast itself. So they stayed in the outer rooms, nibbling at peanuts.

Occasionally they saw others passing by outside, and called them in, telling them about the banquet to which any could come. Many went in and joined the feast as a result, but these others stayed in the outer rooms, having grown accustomed to them now –and went on nibbling at peanuts.

The sounds of people enjoying the feast floated out of the banqueting hall and into the outer rooms. Those still there felt a little bit piqued, that the ones they had invited in were enjoying themselves so much! Their noise disturbed the stillness of the outer rooms. Others wondered what they were making such a song and dance about in there. For although peanuts were of tremendous nutritional value, and they were very grateful for them, it was difficult to get excited about eating them. So, not realising that they now had little appetite for anything else, they went on nibbling peanuts!

©Copyright 1981 Robin Hawkins

The Joy Of My Salvation

Chorus
The joy of my salvation,
Is the joy of knowing You;
Your sweet presence near to me -
Is the strength that holds me true.

When You're near, I see Your hand,
In many little things;
And each moment that I share with You -
Helps my faith grow bigger wings.

That feeling when You're near, Lord,
I want nothing to destroy;
And I'll not flirt with any sin -
That would take away my joy.

When You're near, I'm confident,
I'm following Your Son;
And the things I ask I know You'll grant -
Because our hearts are one.

When You're near, I see so clear,
What things are right and wrong;
And that makes me glad for I'd not do -
Anything to grieve Your Son.

Copyright©1978 Words and Music by Robin Hawkins

You can listen to "The Joy Of My Salvation" at www.robinandjulie.co.uk

Wandsworth Prison Non-Blues

You can take away my freedom,
You can take away my home.
You can take away my family,
And everything I own -

But you can't take away my Jesus,
And He's all I really need.
Even locked up on my own -
Deep inside me I'm freed.

You can take away my baccy,
You can take away my booze.
You can take my local football team,
Especially when they lose -
But you can't take away my Jesus...

If they put me in a prison cell,
And throw away the key.
And everyone forgot me there,
He'd still be near to me -
'Cos you can't take away my Jesus...

Here's everybody longing,
For the day of their release.
No-one wanting to admit,
That day won't bring them peace

Because if you don't know my Jesus
You're still a captive in your soul.
And things won't be no different -
When you get out of this hole!

©Copyright 1982 Words & Music by Robin Hawkins

The tune I use for this song must be the simplest and most unoriginal 12-bar blues ever written! But it works for me, and if you make your own up, I'm sure it would for you as well!

CONVERSATIONS WITH FATHER GOD
"Introspection"

Why can't I love?
Why can't I be loved?
I want to reach out to others,
But in doing so,
I drive them further away.
I want to be surrounded by friends
I want to be loved!

I try to do the right things,
To win people's friendship;
I try to be the person -
They want me to be -
To conform to their expectations.
But it doesn't work –
Anyway, why can't I be loved for myself?

What am I worth to them?
Do they care if I live or die?
I want to be of value to someone
But maybe I put too much value on myself
Maybe "I" keep getting in the way.
I'm not sure that "I" can see further then my eyes!

My Father replied:

This is good, son.
You've started to see -
What makes you unable to see.
When you're wrapped up in how you feel.

What you want
What you need
How will you ever see –
How others feel;
Or understand the things they want or need.
That's the way to be loved:
Create the demand!

But you won't when all you can see is you.
When you stop looking at yourself,
For long enough to look at Me,
You will find a place of security in My love,
From which you will be able -
To reach out to others -
Feeling what they feel
Sensing their needs –
Who knows?
You might just win their friendship too!

Copyright ©1982 Words by Robin Hawkins

He Sent His Son To This

The jolting of a donkey -
Over days of dusty miles.
The would-be mother near her time,
So anxious for her child.
Spurned by those who knew her,
Her disgrace she calmly bore;
Though a child outside of marriage then,
Could mean her death for sure.

Into a world of violence -
Of political intrigue.
A country that was overruled,
By puppet-kings in league -
With occupying armies,
Whose swords were always drawn;
That's the cruel real world -
In which God's Son was born!

So when we sing so glibly,
Songs of joy and cheerfulness;
Just think how much God loved us -
If He sent His Son to this!

Before He learnt to talk -
His life was being hunted down.
Babes in arms were murdered -
Lest He claim an earthly crown!
A fugitive in exile,
A childhood on the run!
Into a world that wished Him dead!
God sent His Royal Son!

So when we sing so glibly....

Rejected by His people -
By the creatures He had made.
They said God's holy, righteous Son,
Received the devil's aid!
But this was just a foretaste -
Of the agony to come;
As whipped and nailed,
He gasped for breath,
As death was overcome.

So when we sing so glibly,
Songs of joy and cheerfulness.
Just think how much God loved us -
If He sent His Son to this!

So let us now sing gladly,
Songs of joy and cheerfulness.
And think how much God loves us -
That He sent His Son to this.

Copyright ©1982 Words & Music by Robin Hawkins

You can listen to "He Sent His Son To This" on www.robinandjulie.co.uk

If I Believed

If I believed what I say I believe,
There'd be nothing that I wouldn't do.
If it would rescue from holocaust fire,
Some people no matter how few.
I'd crawl across miles of barbed wire,
If the deed would get someone reprieved.
T'would be nothing compared with forever,
That is - if I really believed.

If I believed what I say I believe,
There'd be nothing could get in the way.
No tempting distraction, no carnal desire,
There'd be no price that I wouldn't pay.
Who could opt for a brief moment's pleasure-
At the cost of what could be achieved?
And forfeit eternity's treasure,
Not I - if I really believed!

If I believed what I say I believe,
There'd be nothing that I wouldn't be.
I'd be dead to this world, its society twirled -
Round the finger of Lucifer's greed!
And my heart would be filled with a passion,
A constraint beyond any conceived.
To see our God ruling each nation;
That is - if I really believed!

Copyright ©1981 Words & Music by Robin Hawkins

You can listen to "He Sent His Son To This" on www.robinandjulie.co.uk

LOVE
Julie's Song

How would you know that I love you
If I only said it in word?
Could you believe it was real and true
And would your heart then be assured?
But there's more to my love than just saying it;
And it's much more than something I feel.
It's the way that I give you of all that I am -
That will tell you if my love is real.

Love is gentle, so patient and caring,
It looks for the chance to do good.
It accepts what you are without question,
And would share every hurt if it could.
It supports and gives strength in your weakness;
Makes you free to be just what is real.
Love looks at the good that is in you -
And is glad when you say what you feel.

So now you can tell if I love you,
And now you can tell if it's real!
You can rest so secure and so peaceful
If the things that I do – love reveal.
For love needs a means of expression;
And someone to whom it is moved.
And love finds its perfect fulfilment,
If then it in return it is loved.

Copyright ©1981 Words & Music by Robin Hawkins

You can listen to "Julie's Song" on
www.robinandjulie.co.uk.

We've Forgotten How To Die

The world in which we're living's
Grown soft and full of ease;
Cocooned in woolly welfare,
There are few upon their knees.
We want the best from life - Oh yes!
The best that we can buy;
But tragically we lose it,
We've forgotten we must die.

When Jesus walked among us,
And we saw Him thousands feed.
We followed Him readily,
The end to all our need.
He knew our hearts were fickle,
As He looked us in the eye.
And pointed where it mattered,
Saying: "You've got to learn to die!"

A man that's crucified may take
A long, long time to die.
And sin that's only loosely nailed
Is hard to crucify.

Today we are a people
Rarely challenged in our hearts.
To bear a cross as Jesus did –
For that's where His life starts.
No wonder we're so tepid,
Lacking power from on high;
The answer's clear, but painful,
We've forgotten how to die!

Copyright ©1981 Robin Hawkins

Keep The Peace

Let us strive to keep the peace,
Let all pride and anger cease;
Let the harmony of heaven touch our hearts.
As the Spirit is one,
If He's controlling everyone -
We'll be united by the love that He imparts.

We're a long way yet from glory,
When we'll fully grasp the story;
And our clouded eyes at last will clearly see.
But because we've not yet made it,
There'll be times when I'm afraid that -
In our blindness we are going to disagree!

In those times I need the meekness-
Not to hit back when I'm wronged!
And the patience that my Father has with me;
Humility that reckons others better than myself,
And the grace to see how other people feel.

So until that moment's come,
When we've grown up into God's Son;
When we've become united in our faith so sure.
Let us meanwhile keep the peace,
For as these attitudes increase -
His love will bind us all together more and more.

Adapted from Eph4:1-4
Copyright © 1984 Words and music by Robin Hawkins

You can listen to "Keep The Peace" on

www.robinandjulie.co.uk

LOVE
By Your Love

Chorus

By your love will all men know that you're my family;
By your love will people know that you're my Queen.
By the way you show concern for each other they will learn,
How much the least among you means to me.

1. They will see it in the time you give each other,
When much sooner you'd be doing something else.
But how can you learn to care -
Before you've learned the way to share your life,
Love grows from knowing someone really well;

2. They will see it when you share each other's burdens,
Be it just a listening ear or more beside.
The possessions that I lend you -
Will meet all the needs I send you,
No-one need go short or be denied;

Chorus:

3. Love's a fruit that grows from resting in my Spirit;
Love's a fruit that grows and blossoms in its time.
Love is something that you do -
It's got to be a part of you,
But it won't be your love reaching out but mine;

4. It's my love that holds and binds you all together;
It's the hallmark of my Spirit's life in you.
If the world that looks upon you -
Cannot see that love among you,
They've a right to ask if what you've saying is true;

Chorus:
"*By Your love….*

Copyright 1980©Words & Music by Robin Hawkins
You can listen to this song on www.robinandjulie.co.uk.

Nicknames

Let's send our Nicknames back
To where they all belong now,
Old Nick's kept us apart
For far too long now.
In the past, each new division,
Meant another new tradition.
And old Nick's named
Another skirmish won now.

"Divide and conquer" –
That has been his watchword,
To dominate and rule
In times un-numbered.
Often when we've had a scrap,
We've fallen straight into his trap.
Started doing our own thing
For just a wrong word.

Bridge:

If ever there was an abomination,
It's got to be with each denomination.
When each faction says they're right -
But their brother isn't quite!
Then they treat them like they'll get contamination!

These all-embracing names
That some are using,
You'd think that they're
The only ones God's choosing!
There's the Brethren, C of E,
Both are names describing me –
Though I rarely go to either – it's confusing!

Did you hear about the ducks
Fenced off from others?
The pens kept them
From mixing with their brothers.
When the raining didn't stop,
The ducks all floated o'er the top!
Then they all began to swim
With one another!

Bridge

So I'm glad to say such things
Are of the past now,
Each dead tradition's
Disappearing fast now.
When the Spirit sets us free,
His folk are easier to see!
It's good to know that it's as one
That we're all classed now!

Let's send our Nicknames back to where they all belong now,
Old Nick's kept us apart for far too long now.
From now on, we'll stick together,
Be there rain or stormy weather!
And we'll show that in Christ Jesus
We're all one now.

© Copyright 1981 Words & Music by Robin Hawkins

You can listen to "Nicknames" on
www.robinandjulie.co.uk.

Living Word

Chorus
Living Word, my heart bestirred,
I know I heard You speaking.
Living Lord, my heart assured-
And overawed, I'm listening.

You were there right from the start,
The Word in all creation.
Word of God – You lived with us,
You're Jesus – our salvation.

More than merely written word,
More than rules to guide.
The Maker of the Law Himself,
Is standing at my side.

Fresh and clear as mountain stream,
Filled with life and verve.
You spoke right through our endless talk,
And touched that hidden nerve!

Who could keep You, Living Word,
Within the Book's thin pages?
Bursting forth afresh to meet -
The needs of different ages.

Chorus
Living Word, my heart bestirred
I know I heard You speaking;
Living Lord, my heart assured-
And overawed, I'm listening.

Words & Music by Robin Hawkins Copyright ©1981

You can listen to "Living Word" at
www.robinandjulie.co.uk.

Mr. Average

Don't call me Mr. Average,
Nor the man that's in the street.
Don't tell me that I'm normal,
That's an insult quite complete.
For I'm more than just a number,
I'm more than a machine.
I'm a genuine original,
There's no-one quite like me!

You can tell me I'm conceited,
You can tell me that I'm vain.
But God made us each so different,
And He knows us each by name.
Yet Satan tries to spoil -
What God intended we should be;
Just see the ways he steals -
Our individuality!

Chorus: So don't call me Mr Average,

I hope someone finds me special,
Who's prepared to say as much.
My heart responds much more,
When I receive the personal touch.
I need to feel I'm loved -
Without my putting on a sham;
For something in me blooms -
When I'm accepted as I am.

Chorus:

Our God's a God of variety,
Making no two things the same.
Each work of art's original,
And each one bears His Name!
Each blade of grass is different -
Likewise each snowflake too;
But most of all our faces show.
There's no-one quite like you!

Chorus:
So there's no such thing as average,
For each street there's hundred's more.
And "Normal" means my temperature,
Is ninety-eight point four!
I won't be a statistic,
Or a number carefully filed;
I'll be all that God intended -
When He called me as His child.

©Copyright 1980 Words & Music by Robin Hawkins

You can listen to "Don't Call Me Mr Average" at www.robinandjulie.co.uk

Go Free[3]

Tell me how will it be when we're all up yonder,
Standing up before that throne?
There'll be no-one beside you,
There'll be no-one there to guide you -
You'll have never ever been so alone!
You'll have never ever been so alone!

When you're standing up before him,
There'll be no way to ignore Him -
As you've done in all those years back there.
You will see your life reviewed,
And all the time you're wishing you'd -
Paid more attention to the preacher down here!
Paid more attention to the preacher down here!

Then you'll hear that voice -
Like a crash of thunder -
Like a flash of lightning so clear!
To the angel: "Take a look-
See if his name is in the Book"-
If it's not, then you'll be found "Guilty!"
If it's not, then you'll be found "Guilty!"

---

[3] *(Julie & I recorded this song on the day John Lennon was killed! It was an awesome moment when we stopped and realised that if he hadn't already done so, it was too late to put his trust in Jesus to save him.)*

For it could have been so different -
If your life had not been mis-spent -
But you'd taken time to put in your plea.
When condemned for bad behaviour,
You'd be pointing to your Saviour -
And the Judge would now be saying, "Go free!"
Oh yes the Judge would now be saying, "Go free!"

Copyright ©1981 Words & Music by Robin Hawkins

Listen to "Go Free" at www.robinandjulie.co.uk

The Chairman's Song

I'm so glad Lord, You're the King,
Of rain and sunny spells.
And angry waves that pound the shore,
To You are gentle swells.
The air we breathe, is by Your leave,
The wind does what you say.
And nothing can ever happen to me,
Unless you say OK.

So I'll not let things get me down-
Bad times won't make me blue.
But I'll be glad in everything,
And I'll just rest in you.

The cattle on the hills are Yours,
The Bank of England too.
Every power submits to You,
When You should want it to.
You rule my life, its daily chores,
My job by You is run.
So why should I join the union?
When I'm the Chairman's son!

So it don't matter where I am,
For You've promised me You'll lead.
And it don't matter what I have,
For You'll give me all I need.
So I'm just going to seek You, Lord,
Be fulfilled in You alone.
And rest within that peace and joy,
That comes from You alone.

© Copyright 1978 Words & Music Robin Hawkins

You can listen to "The Chairman's Song" at
www.robinandjulie.co.uk

Will You Be My Child?

Will you be my child, will you love Me?
Stretching out your hands, will you trust me?
I want you always there with me,
To share the things I do.
To relax within My love,
Let Me be myself in You;
Me in you; Me in you.

You're more than just a servant,
In duty bound to me.
Obeying Me because you must,
But longing to be free.
For I want to be your Father,
And you be My true son.
To fill your life with streams of love -
That flow back in return.

Will you be my child, will you love Me?
Stretching out your hands, will you trust me?
I want you always there with me,
To share the things I do.
To relax within My love,
Let Me be myself in You;
Me in you; Me in you.

Oh won't you let me set you free,
From all that holds you bound?
To be all that you were meant to be,
And with my life abound.
For only if you love me,
Will you freely come My way;
And only if you love Me,
Will you gladly Me obey.

©Copyright 1978 Words & Music by Robin Hawkins
You can listen to "Will you be my child? At
www.robinandjulie.co.uk

Getting Younger

Chorus:

Oh I know I'm getting younger every day!
Growing down more like a child in every way.
Yet though my body's older,
And my hair has gone all grey -
Well, I still feel I'm getting younger every day.

It's strange how when I started out -
I thought I knew so much.
But only those who are old and wise -
Can ever be as such.
Now as the days roll into years,
My knowledge pales away,
As in my sight You larger grow -
A little more each day!

And at the start I really knew -
So little of Your love.
But with the passing of the years -
I found how deep it was.
Now I'm basking in the sunshine,
Of Your love so real,
And when Your Spirit lifts my heart -
I so much younger feel!

Have you ever seen a tiny child
Reach out in simple trust?
It's sad to see it fade in time -
But grow I suppose they must.
With wavering trust, I met my Lord,
So many years ago,
But now just like that tiny child's-
I see it daily grow!

So many people seem to fear -
The passing of the years.
And all their time is spent -
In trying to keep away grey hairs!
But if only they knew of,
This life that's just begun.
For when this body's due for scrap -
I'll get a brand new one!
Chorus

©Copyright 1978 Words & Music by Robin Hawkins

You can listen to "Getting Younger" At www.robinandjulie.co.uk.

__His Name Is I Am__

So many live on memories,
That happened long ago.
Others on a touch of God -
That filled them once aglow.
We say they were the good old days,
They could have been and yet.
Time sweetens bitter memories,
And helps us them forget.

But His Name is "I Am"-
Ever since time began,
Not I was, or I will be, or I may.
It's this point in time that's important, and I'm –
Not concerned with what may come or yesterday.

Regrets and disappointments,
Things that happened long ago.
Will keep us from enjoying life -
If we'll not let them go.
Forget the things that might have been,
Can't change them anyhow.
The only thing that God's concerned with's,
Where we are right now.

Some are always dreaming,
Building castles in the sky.
While looking to the future -
Life is passing them on by.
Always looking hopeful,
Always hoping for that break;
Their life is built on chances,
Gambling with each choice they make.

Chorus: But His Name is "I Am"-
Ever since time began,
Not I was, or I will be, or I may.
It's this point in time that's important, and I'm –
Not concerned with what may come or yesterday.

©Copyright 1981 Words & Music by Robin Hawkins

You can listen to "His Name Is I Am" At
www.robinandjulie.co.uk

Martha, Mary

Martha, Martha, much to do,
The day's work to be done.
"Hi, Lord, Bye Lord" 's all the time-
She's spending with Your Son!
No matter, all the work she does,
It's You she's trying to please.
Let her finish, then you'll see-
How good a girl she is.

Busy in Your work, I'm busy,
Doing so much for You.
So little time is there to stop -
The things I'm trying to do!
Yet I hear You call me,
Over the hustle of each day.
"Stop what you're doing,
Stop where you're going -
And quietly come away."

Mary, Mary, not contrary,
Waiting at Your feet.
The world could stop,
And she'd get off,
With You her life's so sweet.
Though there's always such a lot,
To keep her from Your side.
There's one thing that's essential-
You'll make sure she's not denied.

So let my heart be still,
And let me listen to You, Lord.
Let me know Your peace,
and let me rest within You Lord.
In the busy life I lead,
There seems so little time to spare.
Yet You can speak only when I am -
Still enough to hear.

©Copyright 1980 Words & Music by Robin Hawkins

You can listen to "Martha, Mary" At www.robinandjulie.co.uk

Talking Evolution Blues

Three or four hundred years ago,
When people's knowledge began to grow,
There was a group raised in defiance -
A brand new god - and called it Science.
Among them Darwin said he thought -
We'd come from apes - that's what he taught!
His friends declared, "That might be odd -
If we're from apes, then who needs God -
To show us how the world was made.
It's obvious now." - Or so they said.
After all, they were around at the time.
And God wasn't?

So now we're teaching kids in schools,
That we've outgrown God's golden rules.
He didn't give us hearts like his,
But ones like monkeys in the trees -
A more developed counterpart -
But still an animal at heart.
- No wonder kids behave like them!

We've got this thing called carbon-dating-
Latest thing in estimating,
Tells us that some stony fossil's
Got an age that's quite colossal!
But then a living snail was told,
"You're one million and two years old!"
Happy Birthday!
Ah well, can't be right all the time!

If things are as old as the age they say-
A million years as a passing day!
I'm told that the moon that's up there must -
Be buried deep in cosmic dust.
A bit each year since long ago,
Should mean there's 60ft or so -
Of stardust - all over the moon.

So here's our spacemen off the plane,
Landed safe on earth again,
Asked, "Was it deep - just like we guessed?
Said, "No - there's just three feet or less!"

Back to the drawing board again!

We've got this law called Entropery
Works against this Evo theory;
It shows us that we face decay -
Declining fast, wrinkled and gray!
We don't get better, just get weak -
Like cars that rust, we're back to dust,
For life's dissolving, not evolving
Nature has its way.

Funny how Father God's been
changed for Mother Nature!

Trouble is, this evo theory -
Needed evidence to veri-
Fy its truth for all to see -
"Don't worry, it's not going to be -
Too long before we get the facts -
Then we can really put the axe -
To Genesis!"

It's still here. So is Entropy!
How's the evidence doing?

Truth is, much of what's been found-
Does not confirm what they expound.
And so, because facts fail to fit,
They get discarded bit by bit.
But gradually they've been gaining weight -
'Til someone, somewhere said, "Hey wait! -
Life would be great and hunky dory -
If we could discard this Darwin story!

Oh Oh! If we did that, then we're afraid,
We'd have to admit the world was made!

©Copyright 1982 Words by Robin Hawkins

You can listen to "Talkin' Evolution Blues" at www.robinandjulie.co.uk.

The Prickly Hedge

There's some like country western,
And others like The Dales.
Still more like good old glory songs -
And others hymns from Wales.
Some think to praise with one accord –
-ian is quite enough!
But who will tell me what the Lord -
Would like to hear from us.

We're called to be an Olive tree,
Not a prickly hedge!
So never let the way we sing
Become a driving wedge.
The outward patterns matter less -
Than love that knows no guile;
And that gives Father much more joy
Than any form or style.

Though some like country western,
Though some still like The Dales.
Though some like good old glory songs
And still more, hymns from Wales!
There's many other instruments -
From Whistle to Bassoon.
But dreadful is their sound, if with –
Each other they're off-tune!

If you want the best for all
This thing called *agape,*
Then sing the songs your brother likes,
Then what *you* like, he'll play.
This shows care for others as,
We praise with hearts in tune.
And Father will be thrilled, in fact –
He'll be over the moon!

We'll still like Country Western.
We still can like The Dales.
We still can like those glory songs,
And even hymns from Wales!
Guitars can play with one accord-
-ian, and still want more!
Thus Jesus gets more glory
Than He ever did before!

©Copyright 1985 Words by Robin Hawkins

Walk On The Water

Chorus:

Walk on the water,
Run o'er the sea.
Leave the shore behind you,
Move out o'er the deep.
Walk on the water,
Run o'er the sea.
Don't look at the wind and waves -
Look into my face.

I see You, Jesus -
On the water,
Beckoning to me.
I see the longing in Your eyes,
To come and set me free.
As a child that learns to walk -
Must take his Father's hand;
So Jesus I reach out to You,
Please help me to stand.

Chorus:

Sometimes I'm afraid to follow,
Places that You go.
I cling so hard to what I see,
Trust in things I know.
I'd feel much safer in a boat,
Or close in to the land,
With something firm beneath my feet,
But the shore's just made of sand!

Chorus:
                Of course the waves aren't really waves,
                It's not the wind that blows.
                I see You only in my heart,
                It's there Your presence grows.
                But the doubts and trials are real enough,
                The world throws out its lure.
                My selfish heart would have its way,
                I need Your Spirit's power!

©Copyright 1977 Words & Music by Robin Hawkins

You can listen to "Walk On The Water" at www.RobinandJulie.co.uk

Things Start Happening

Chorus:
Things start happening when God is in our midst,
Things start happening when we do as He bids.
And when we open up our hearts, and seek His will each day,
Then we'll find things start happening in the most amazing way.

It blows my mind to know You've plans -
In which I've got a place.
And more to know that You control -
This wilful human race.
There's more You want to give and do -
Than ever I'd conceive.
There's never been a tangle yet -
You couldn't still unweave.

Your timing Lord is perfect -
When required, You're always there.
And intricate arrangements -
Simply show another flair.
In engineering situations,
You just pull the strings.
And while Your children play their part
You're watching from the wings.

There's just one thing that grieves me -
And it hurts me deep inside.
To think of all you could have done-
Had it not been for my pride.
I'm afraid that things won't happen,
So afraid I'll look a fool!
But all you need is someone-
Who's prepared to be that fool.

©Copyright 1980 Words & Music by Robin Hawkins

You can listen to "Things Start Happening" At www.RobinandJulie.co.uk

Still The Hungry Die

See the granaries filled with grain,
See more truck-loads come by train.
Now new barns they build again,
    But still the Hungry die!

See the butter-mountain growing,
Dumps of fruit and veg bulldozing.
Fish thrown back and we full-knowing,
    That the Hungry die!

Don't tell me that you didn't see,
They're always showing it on TV.
You're to blame as much as me!
    But they're the ones to die!

You say the world's too populated,
    Let a famine dissipate it.
As long as we've got adequate -
    It matters not who dies!

It's not as if there's insufficient,
Food for all, we're just inefficient.
Selfish, greedy, high-ambitioned,
    Liking our life-style!

Instead we hear the market's cry,
We've got to keep the prices high.
Don't be dumb, start asking why -
    It's all for you and I!

Why not admit you just don't care?
You know that it's not really fair.
Yet it's the Lord we'd better fear!
When He starts asking "Why?"

There must be something we can give,
To help these people start to live.
Apathy's hard to forgive,
Concern is just the start.

One voice may not make much sound,
With ten it starts to get around.
A thousand really shakes the ground -
P'raps then we'll hear their cry!

©Copyright 1982 Words & Music by Robin Hawkins

Talking Hey Bert's Got Religion Blues

Hey Bert, you know old Alfie Tubb -
The one what played darts down the pub.
Well I saw 'im today, and 'e gimme a nod,
Here, you know what Bert, 'e's joined God-squad
You should have 'eard 'im go on;
Summat about 'ow 'e was a Christian
'E was all elo… elo… elo.. eloquick?
Oh 'ell I dunno, 'e was full of long words!

'E said 'e'd got a life that's new -
'Is past forgotten, 'is worries too!
'E said in Jesus, 'e'd a friend -
Y'know the sort on whom you can depend
Then 'e said ''e wouldn't die,
But'd live forever with God on high!

'N I'll be damned! Ever been 'ad?
Sounds like someone's taken 'im to the cleaners

Well it didn't worry me wot 'e chose to think;
So I said, "Come on down we'll 'ave a drink.
But wot 'e said next really took some beating!
'E was already going to a prayer meeting!
Prayer-Meeting!?
I never knew that bloke refuse a trip to the
boozer yet!
'N 'ere 'e was going to a "prayer meeting"!
I thought, "Poor bloke!" 'e's really got it bad this time!

An' I laughed at that till m'sides near split me;
Thought for a minute 'e were gonna 'it me.
But 'e didn't do a thing, just stood there smiling,
Looked sorta iyuck, like someone's darling!

I thought aaaah – 'e's gone all soft,
'E just wants a good spot of bovver!
Then e'll be alright, won't 'e?

You know it got my goat t'see the change in 'im,
I'd prove 'e weren't no saint – if 'e 'it my chin!
Well y'know what it's like when a mate goes wrong,
You've to bring 'im back where 'e belongs.
Even if it does cost you a black eye or two.

Well I swore at 'im wi' every thing I knew;
Slapped 'is mouth, made it black 'n blue.
But 'e give me a look that cut me thro, it did,
'E smiled 'n said, "God loves you too, Sid!" *God lo…me?*
Y'know I couldn't say a bloomin' thing
I just stood there – speechless. Felt like I'd done somethin'
rotten
'N wanted to say "sorry"; but I couldn't get it out.
Well, 'e walked off then, 'n left me there,

Still smiling like 'e 'ad no care!
I dunno wot's making 'im act so strange,
But that Alfie bloke's completely changed!
'E's not the one I used to know anyway.
It's 'ard to put your finger on it,
But 'e seems much 'appier now
And 'is eyes – there's a peace there somehow.
Makes you think, dunnit?
Here Bert, do you reckon there's anything in this
Christianity lark?

© Copyright 1970 Robin Hawkins

You can listen to "Talkin' Hey Bert" at
www.RobinandJulie.co.uk.

Gentle Waters

Gentle waters, freely flowing,
Crystal clear, so bright and glowing.
Wash me 'til no stain is showing,
What I used to be.

Wash the sin so overpowering,
Wash the guilt that leaves me cowering;
Bedew the bud so newly flowering,
In your light of day.

I've always walked on solid ground,
Wanting to be safe and sound;
But now I want my old life drowned,
In your floods of grace.

To live I need the art of dying,
All of me needs crucifying;
Then I'll rise with wings a-flying,
Soaring to the skies.

So let me here right now be counted,
Firmly in your word be planted.
Every obstacle surmounted,
As I walk with you.

©Copyright 1981 Words and Music by Robin Hawkins

You can listen to "Gentle Waters" at
www.RobinandJulie.co.uk

The Barrel Song

Have you ever known the joy of having nothing?
Do you know the joy of working with the Lord?
Don't you know your Father's riches are at your command?
To meet your every need, they'll be outpoured!
Don't worry, Father's bank account can stand it.
To Him the Bank of England's petty cash;
You can hang on to your wallet, but you'll never know the way
God gives with so much freedom and panache!

Chorus:
Take me to the bottom of the barrel!
Let me run on 'til I'm out of steam.
Take me to the bottom of the barrel,
To know just what "Rock-bottom" really means!
I need to come to the end of my resources,
Be even on occasion down and out!
For when I'm bottom of the barrel,
Only then can I draw cheques on God's account.

It's no use hanging onto little nest-eggs,
It's no use saving for a rainy day.
If you ever want to draw on Heaven's overflowing store-
You're going to have to learn to give it all away!
If you don't, the barrel's bottom grows elastic;
You've always got a little, just in case…
And a little's all you'll have for ever after
For it's only empty barrels Heaven pays.

It's no use running round in circles,
Showing God the way things really should be run.
There's no point in drawing up ideas and plans -
If we only ask His blessing when it's done!
What would take us months to do takes Him 5 minutes!
And the job will last much longer, yes it will;
So why do we keep going 'til we're exhausted?
God can do it so much easier when we're still.

©Copyright 1980 Words & Music by Robin Hawkins

You can listen to "The Barrel Song" at "www.RobinandJulie.co.uk

It's So Good

Chorus
It's so good, Lord to be here,
To gather at Your feet.
It's so good, Lord to be here,
To feel Your warmth so sweet.

As we wait, Lord, in the stillness,
There're no words that need be said.
Lifting hands in gentle worship,
Up to You, our living Head.

May the thoughts we have be Yours, Lord,
Our ideas and burdens too.
May everything we do, Lord,
Find its origin in You.

Please open up our hearts,
And our ears to all You're saying.
To be united in Your will,
For Your vision, Lord, we're praying.

©Copyright 1981 Words and Music by Robin Hawkins

You can listen to "It's So Good" at
www.RobinandJulie.co.uk

So much to sing

We've got so much that we want to sing about,
So much that we want to share!
When we count up every blessing,
We just have to keep expressing,
All His greatness, all his goodness, all His care!
We've got so much that we want to sing about,
So much that we want to share!
Because our God's alive and active!
His love is so attractive.
We'll sing the songs He gives us everywhere.

When by Satan I get told -
That my songs are getting old,
And there's not too many new ones on the way!
I start counting one by one
All the things that God has done
And the devil pretty quickly runs away!

We find there's so much that we want to sing about,
So much that we want to share;
When we count up every blessing,
We just have to keep expressing
All His greatness, all His goodness, all His care.

I'm forgiven by my Saviour,
And He's promised His behaviour,
By His Spirit's gentle power will shine on through!
He has promised me His glory,
By believing in His story,
And by walking in His ways in all I do.

Now there's so much that we want to sing about,
So much that we want to share!
Because our God's alive and active!
His love is so attractive,
We'll sing the songs He gives us everywhere.

So when you feel depressed and blue
Now you'll know just what to do,
Don't you let them devils steal away your joy
If, in all things you keep praising,
You will find it quite amazing
There's contentment in your heart
They can't destroy!
You'll have so much that you'll want to
Sing about
So much that you want to share!
Because our God's alive and active!
His love is so attractive.
We'll sing the songs He gives us
We'll sing the songs He gives us
We'll sing the songs He gives us
everywhere !

© Copyright 1981 Words and music by Robin Hawkins

You can listen to "So Much To Sing" at www.RobinandJulie.co.uk

You Were Made For Me

You were made for Me, Oh can't you see -
That you'll never be free on your own.
Can't you see that I long to satisfy,
The deepest desires of your soul.

You're made with a God-shaped hole in your heart -
That can only be filled by Me.
How long will you go on hurting yourself,
Not so liberated or free.

I know you're trying to find, a little peace of mind -
Of the kind only found in Me.
It's an endless quest, with your life a mess,
'Til you find your rest in Me.

Bridge:

Your words are profound-
But your head's in the ground,
And you never think anything through.
To every straw you cling, believing anything,
Before accepting My claims on you!

You were made for Me, Oh can't you see -
That you'll never be free on your own.
Can't you see that I long to satisfy,
The deepest desires of your soul.

© Copyright 1980 Words and music by Robin Hawkins

You can listen to "You Were Made For Me" at www.RobinandJulie.co.uk

A Gentle Plea For Tolerance

Oh please will you be patient,
God's not finished with me yet.
It's going to be a life-long work,
If me He will perfect.
But He's promised He'll complete it-
He's working overtime;
And all you'll see will be Jesus then -
Just His life, none of mine!

I know it seems if you look at me,
He's not got very far,
But I'm so glad that you can't see
,Just where He had to start
For I know I'm far from perfect -
And in fact I'm pretty raw;
Still I know the Lord's improved on me,
From what I was before.

There've been times I've tried to help him,
But I just got in the way.
I tried to do what I thought was right ,
Like acting in a play.
Then I stopped wrestling, started nestling -
Now my spirit's free;
And with His law within my heart,
His life comes naturally.

© Copyright 1978 Words and Music by Robin Hawkins

You can listen to "A Gentle Plea For Tolerance" at www.RobinandJulie.co.uk

The Bride

I have seen nothing quite so beautiful
As that which was created for one already so.
But, supposing we,
With all the gathered skill of years,
Set out to build a work of art
To be the crown of all creation!
What would it be?
A computer with the capacity of the human brain?
A piece of sculpture – with the fine detail of a tree
A concrete edifice – with the majesty of Everest?
What could it be?
We, whose finest efforts only ever show
How greater far is the Creator!
Let us concede defeat - and admit Him
Our Master!
Now! Stand aside and watch as He, the Master
Builds His Masterpiece:
The crown to His creation!
Watch as He explores our need:
Studies our every desire, and every longing
To find the perfect complement
See the beauty in His work
Perfection in the finest detail!
No, I have seen nothing quite so beautiful
Quite so fair and lovely
As that which was created: woman
To be a bride.

©Copyright 1970 Written by Robin Hawkins

Notes:
If you want to find out more about becoming a Christian, and a follower of Jesus, then go to www.EveryStudent.com

europe books